K

M000114720

Reading Standards for Literature

Patricia Pavelka

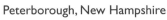

Professional Development
SDE Resources

Peterborough, New Hampshire

Husky Trail Press LLC

East Lyme, Connecticut

Published by:

Staff Development for Educators (SDE)
10 Sharon Road, PO Box 500
Peterborough, NH 03458
1-800-321-0401
www.SDE.com/crystalsprings

and

Husky Trail Press LLC
PO Box 705
East Lyme, CT 06333
1-860-739-7644
www.huskytrailpress.com

Published 2013

Printed in the United States of America

17 16 15 14 13   1 2 3 4 5

ISBN: 978-1-935502-70-8

e-book ISBN: 978-1-935502-71-5

Contents

Dedication

To
Beatrice DeGruttola

for all the time and dedication you put forth in caring for all those four-legged friends who need help. I can't begin to thank you for making our house a home. My family and I have truly been blessed to have you, and the dogs you have entrusted to us, in our lives.

Acknowledgments

I am grateful to:

Mom. You taught me life's greatest lessons.

Lois Schenking. You are unmatched as an editor. You're always here for me at a moment's notice. You work diligently through the wee hours of the night, and I truly appreciate everything you do.

Jo-Ann Geida. You are always there through thick and thin. I can never thank you enough for all of the different things you are to me: cousin, friend, neighbor, office manager, traveling buddy . . . just to name a few.

Staff Development for Educators. Thank you for the enormous amount of time and dedication you put into supporting our educators. Almost 20 years ago you published my first book. Thank you for starting me on my journey as an author. I'm looking forward to working together on our future endeavors. Thank you, **Lisa Bingen** and **Sharon Smith,** for seeing the vision of this Common Core series and for the hard work you put in to make it a reality. Thank you, **Deborah Fredericks,** for the production and organization. Thank you, **Roberta Bell**, for all the hard work you've done as project manager. **Cheryl Simmons,** I appreciate all the support you've given me throughout our years together.

Noel Sorensen. Thank you for your endless fires, meals, and patience as this manuscript was evolving.

Our Teachers and Educators. You've invited me to teach with you, work side by side with your students, exchange ideas, and share children's work. It is an honor to be a part of your educational walk.

Richard LaPorta. Your belief in me is the greatest gift I could receive. Thank you for always being a part of these writing endeavors. You have an incredible talent for seeing plain text and turning it into a work of art.

Introduction

This book is designed to help educators explore and effectively implement the Common Core Reading Standards for Literature, specifically at the kindergarten level. Included are open-ended assignments, centers, and activities to use with almost any book or text on a daily basis. You will find instructional strategies and activities that support student engagement with the standards. Our goal as educators is to support and challenge students in applying deeper thinking and rigor as they work with these standards. There are many resources available for explaining the emergence of the Common Core State Standards (CCSS), as well as resources that give specific activities to go along with specific books. The goal of this resource is to give kindergarten teachers ideas that can be used throughout the whole year with just about any book as they work on a daily basis with concepts that are included in the CCSS.

This book does not have to be read in order from cover to cover. At the top of each page is a banner, which is a quick reference to tell you which standard is being addressed. By looking at the banners, you can go directly to the pages that have strategies and activities for a specific standard.

The book is organized into five parts.

PART I focuses on the category Key Ideas and Details, College and Career Readiness Anchor Standards 1 through 3, and specific kindergarten competencies designated for this anchor standard.

CATEGORY	**Anchor Standards**	**Kindergarten**
KEY IDEAS AND DETAILS	**1.** Read closely to determine what the text says explicitly and to make logical inferences from it; cite specific textual evidence when writing or speaking to support conclusions drawn from the text.	**RL.K.1** With prompting and support, ask and answer questions about key details in a text.
	2. Determine central ideas or themes of a text and analyze their development; summarize the key supporting details and ideas.	**RL.K.2** With prompting and support, retell familiar stories, including key details.
	3. Analyze how and why individuals, events, and ideas develop and interact over the course of a text.	**RL.K.3** With prompting and support, identify characters, settings, and major events in a story.

PART 2 focuses on the category Craft and Structure, College and Career Readiness Anchor Standards 4 through 6, and specific kindergarten competencies designated for this anchor standard.

CATEGORY	Anchor Standards	Kindergarten
CRAFT AND STRUCTURE	**4.** Interpret words and phrases as they are used in a text, including determining technical, connotative, and figurative meanings, and analyze how specific word choices shape meaning or tone.	**RL.K.4** Ask and answer questions about unknown words in a text.
	5. Analyze the structure of texts, including how specific sentences, paragraphs, and larger portions of the text (e.g., a section, chapter, scene, or stanza) relate to each other and the whole.	**RL.K.5** Recognize common types of texts (e.g., storybooks, poems).
	6. Assess how point of view or purpose shapes the content and style of a text.	**RL.K.6** With prompting and support, name the author and illustrator of a story and define the role of each in telling the story.

PART 3 focuses on the category Integration of Knowledge and Ideas, College and Career Readiness Anchor Standards 7 and 9, and specific kindergarten competencies designated for this anchor standard.

CATEGORY	Anchor Standards	Kindergarten
INTEGRATION OF KNOWLEDGE AND IDEAS	**7.** Integrate and evaluate content presented in diverse media and formats, including visually and quantitatively, as well as in words.	**RL.K.7** With prompting and support, describe the relationship between illustrations and the story in which they appear (e.g., what moment in a story an illustration depicts).
	8. Not applicable to literature.	**RL.K.8** Not applicable to literature.
	9. Analyze how two or more texts address similar themes or topics in order to build knowledge or to compare the approaches the authors take.	**RL.K.9** With prompting and support, compare and contrast the adventures and experiences of characters in familiar stories.

PART 4 focuses on the category Range of Reading and Level of Text Complexity, College and Career Readiness Anchor Standard 10, and specific kindergarten competencies designated for this anchor standard.

CATEGORY	Anchor Standards	Kindergarten
RANGE OF READING AND LEVEL OF TEXT COMPLEXITY	**10.** Read and comprehend complex literary and informational texts independently and proficiently.	**RL.K.10** Actively engage in group reading activities with purpose and understanding.

PART 5 looks at formative assessments that can be used on a daily basis while working in a whole-group setting. They are easy to implement and keep us aware of specific students' needs as we are in the midst of teaching. These assessments do not replace the individual assessments needed and required to inform us about what reading levels are appropriate for students. Running records and specific reading assessments are an integral part of assessing student performance and achievement.

Students will need explicit instruction in all of the strategies and ideas presented in this book. To show or model how to do something once will not lead students to become independent, high-level thinkers. In Richard Cash's book *Advancing Differentiation: Thinking and Learning for the 21st Century,* the author argues that partially implementing new ideas won't make a huge difference. He explains they must be implemented to a high degree to be successful. Malcolm Gladwell, in his book *Outliers*, talks about expertise requiring an investment of ten thousand hours. Can you imagine the expertise of readers in our country given ten thousand hours of reading practice?

Throughout this book you will see initials such as RL.K.1. This refers to Reading Literature, Kindergarten level, Standard 1. Another example is RL.K.6, which refers to Reading Literature, Kindergarten level, Standard 6.

As we work through this information, we need to be aware of the broader Common Core anchor standards, as well as the kindergarten grade-level-specific standards. Also included are first-grade competency standards, as some students may benefit from working beyond kindergarten level.

Key Ideas and Details
Anchor Standards 1–3
RL.K.1–3

This category of Key Ideas and Details requires, first of all, that students comprehend literally and know what the text says explicitly. Secondly, students must be able to make inferences. In both cases, using textual support to back up answers is required. Common Core is requiring that our youngest readers attend to comprehension and read closely.

Standard 1. *Read closely to determine what the text says explicitly and to make logical inferences from it; cite specific textual evidence when writing or speaking to support conclusions drawn from the text.*

Kindergarten (RL.K.1)

With prompting and support, ask and answer questions about key details in a text.

Grade 1 (RL.1.1)

Ask and answer questions about key details in a text.

As students read and answer questions about the text, the goal is to get them back into the book and citing specific textual evidence to back up their answers. We are asking kindergartners to tell us what the text says and implies.

Answering Questions About Key Details

Most of the time, when asking questions about key details in a text, we should be marking and posting students' answers directly in the text. For example, after the teacher read the book titled *Victor* to the class, students were asked the question: How does Victor feel about living in the city and why? The following text and illustrations were highlighted as we discussed this question, and these explanations were given for the highlighted parts.

1. Victor must like it in the city because he has a family. He has a bed to sleep in now and is not outside in the cold.

Victor lived alone in a busy city.

One chilly day a family found Victor and took him home.

2. He must like it in the city because he has friends. And if you have friends, then you have someone to play with, and you can have fun.

3. This is easy because it says right here, "Life was great."

4. Look at Victor's face. He is smiling, so he must be happy.

5. The spotty dog wants him to come out and play, so he must be happy. He doesn't have to sit home alone and be bored with nothing to do.

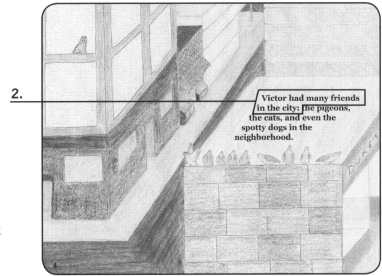

2.

Victor had many friends in the city: the pigeons, the cats, and even the spotty dogs in the neighborhood.

The goal is to have students refer to the text to support their thoughts and answers. In this example, students answered questions by:

determining what the text said explicitly (number 3)

making logical inferences (numbers 1 & 2)

citing specific textual evidence (numbers 1 & 2)

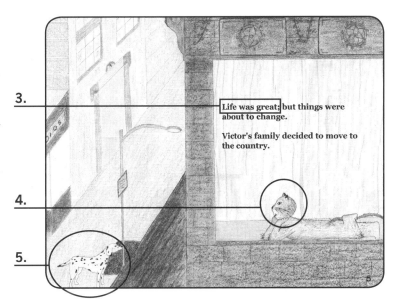

3.

Life was great, but things were about to change.

Victor's family decided to move to the country.

4.

5.

Notice also how other standards were integrated with this activity. RL.K.7 was addressed in this example, as students used the illustrations to back up some of their thoughts. Students pointed out that Victor was smiling in the picture, so he must be happy and content (number 4). They also noticed the illustration of the spotty dog in the street looking up at Victor in the window. They concluded that the dog wanted Victor to come out and play, therefore giving Victor something fun to do instead of being at home alone and bored.

Question Prompts

We want our students asking and answering questions about things explicitly stated in the text, as well as ones that promote higher-level thinking and discussions. Students need much modeling and scaffolding in order to ask thought-provoking questions. This activity reinforces the same prompts for any book. The more students hear and use these prompts, the more the prompts will become internalized. The goal is to get students to ask themselves questions *as* they are reading or listening to a story.

Below are questions for each question word. Some are based on what the text says explicitly; others require students to make logical inferences. Also there are some broad, open-ended questions. In all discussions, students need to be able to cite textual evidence.

Who

Although most of these question prompts do not start with the word "who," they are inquiries about the "who" (characters) in the text.

Who is the main character? How would you describe him/her?

How is _____ feeling? Why?

Do you like _____? Why? Why not?

Do you think _____ behaved responsibly? Why? Why not?

What did _____ do . . . ?

What

What if . . . ?

What happened in the story?

What do you think about . . . ?

What made _____ decide to . . . ?

What part of the book/story was most interesting or surprising? Why?

What would be another good title for this story? Why?

Where

Where does the story take place?

Where did _____ learn a life lesson in the story?

Where were you confused in the story? Why?

Where in the story did the character get what he/she deserved? Why?

Where in the story was the problem beginning to be solved? Where was it finally solved?

When

When did the problem get solved?

When did you want to have an argument with _____?

When did you disagree with _____? Why?

When did you agree with _____? Why?

When did . . . ?

When would you have asked _____ to . . . ?

Why

Why do you think . . . ?

Why does _____ feel . . . ?

Why did _____ say . . . ?

Why did _____ do . . . ?

Why did _____ choose . . . ?

Would you recommend this book to a friend? Why? Why not?

How

How would . . . ?

How have _____ feelings changed? Why?

How do the characters relate to each other?

How does _____ change in the story?

How does the setting affect the plot of the story?

Remember, the goal of these prompts is to use them as a springboard for discussions and to help students begin to have their own queries. The intention is not for students to memorize and use only these specific prompts. Other resources for questioning include:

Critical Thinking Wheels. Houston, TX: Mentoring Minds.

Pavelka, Patricia. *Question Prompts: Taking Comprehension to a Higher Level.* East Lyme, CT: Husky Trail Press LLC.

Quick Flip Questions for Critical Thinking Based on Bloom's Taxonomy. Madison, WI: Edupress.

Quick Flip Questions for the Revised Bloom's Taxonomy. Madison, WI: Edupress.

Webb, Dr. Norman. *Depth of Knowledge—Descriptors, Examples and Question Stems for Increasing Depth of Knowledge in the Classroom.* Madison, WI: Wisconsin Center for Education Research.

We must ask students to explain their thinking! Use follow-up statements or questions for deeper thinking.

Tell me more.

Why do you think that?

Can you support your answer?

How did you get to that answer?

What in the text helped you come to that answer?

Explain your thinking.

As students are having text-centered conversations, we expect them to listen to each other and respond to comments and opinions.

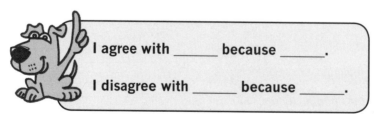

I agree with _____ because _____.

I disagree with _____ because _____.

Question Critters

Give students tongue depressors and have them create critters. They can use wiggly eyes, markers, glitter, pipe cleaners, etc. Make sure they only decorate one side of each tongue depressor.

Copy the reproducibles on pages 76–78, cut out the question prompts, and glue them onto the blank sides of the tongue depressors.

Copy the apple reproducibles on pages 79–81 to wrap around individual student-sized milk cartons. Make six homes for the question critters: who, what, where, why, when, and how. Below are examples of the "who" and "where" homes.

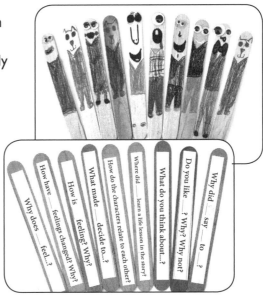

Students take turns choosing a critter and asking a question based on the prompt. They can either answer the question themselves or ask someone in the class to answer. If they choose to have someone other than themselves answer the question, then they must repeat the answer. I usually find my stronger learners want to ask and answer the questions themselves. My struggling learners want to ask the question but have someone else answer it. That's fine to begin with as long as they repeat the question and the answer. Repeating makes them attentive to the answer and also increases their comprehension as high-level questions and answers are modeled.

Modeling with Question Prompts

These question prompts must be modeled many times in whole-class settings and small groups before students can begin to internalize the prompts and use them independently.

Practice using each of the prompts as questions specific to many different stories. Students will see how one question prompt can be used for just about any text.

Below are examples of using this "when" prompt with different stories: When did _____ have an "ah-ha" moment?

When did Clifford have an "ah-ha" moment?

When did Toad have an "ah-ha" moment?

When did Wilbur have an "ah-ha" moment?

Below are examples of using this "how" prompt with different stories: How have _____ feelings changed? Why?

How have the kittens' feelings toward Victor changed since they found out why he hissed at them? Why did that change their feelings for him?

How did Victor's feelings about living in the city change after the kittens visited him at his house? Why did his feelings about the city then change?

Below are examples of using this "why" prompt with different stories: Why do you think . . . ?

Why do you think Hansel and Gretel dropped crumbs as they were walking through the woods?

Why do you think the kittens do not want to play with Victor?

Why do you think Emily Elizabeth wants to have a surprise party for Clifford?

I Wonder Wheel

Copy the reproducible on page 82 and glue it onto a piece of posterboard. Attach a paper arrow with a brad as a spinner.

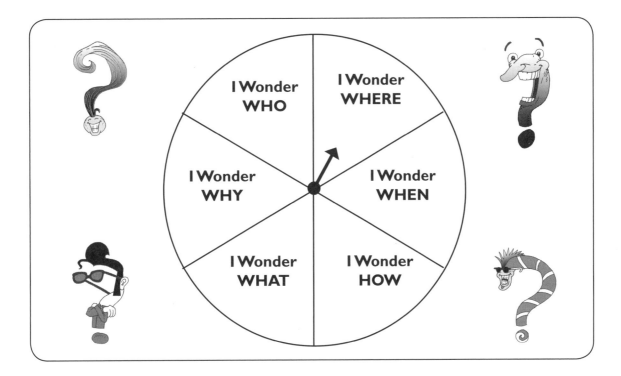

This *I Wonder Wheel* is used during whole-group and guided reading group lessons. Students take turns spinning the arrow and asking questions based on where the arrow lands.

Cris Tovani talks about the relationship between questioning and inferring. "Expecting students to infer before they question a text is unreasonable. Inferential thinking is born out of questions the reader has about information stated indirectly in the text. Inferences are found in the reader's head. Questioning helps readers go beyond literal meaning in order to engage in inferential thinking."

Part 1
KEY IDEAS AND DETAILS

Standard 2. *Determine central ideas or themes of a text and analyze their development; summarize the key supporting details and ideas.*

Kindergarten (RL.K.2)

With prompting and support, retell familiar stories, including key details.

Grade 1 (RL.1.2)

Retell stories, including key details, and demonstrate understanding of their central message or lesson.

As students retell stories, we see their organization of ideas and comprehension of the story. Retellings help internalize story elements. As students practice retelling of multiple stories many times, they begin to see the story elements of characters, settings, and events as parts of all stories. They learn to begin their retellings with setting and characters. They continue with initial problems and events that are happening. They retell the events in order and understand that each story has a beginning, middle, and end. With daily practice, we begin to see an increase in explicit story recall, as well as development of story and character interpretations.

Retelling builds story language and story patterns: Once upon a time . . . lived happily ever after . . . decided to go out and seek their fortune. It expands and develops oral language and encourages confidence in speaking.

Retellings can be used as assessment tools. They tell us:

- What a student remembers
- What a student thinks is important to remember: key details told or left out
- How a student sequences information
- How a student organizes information
- A student's ability to infer
- A child's overall comprehension of a story
- A child's knowledge of story elements—especially characters, setting, and events
- The language development of a student

Storyboards

Storyboards are a way of retelling whereby students create the setting and make paper puppets to aid their comprehension. Storyboards give students props and visuals to help organize and internalize the story. Following are examples.

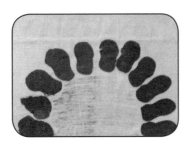

Three Billy Goats Gruff

Kindergartners are usually given something to use for their storyboards. It is their choice whether they use the item or not. The child who completed the sample to the left wanted to make his own bridge. He did not use the cutout provided. In the sample to the right, the child chose to use the bridge provided.

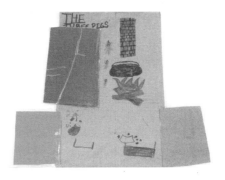

Three Little Pigs

Under each of the three "doors," the student drew the inside of the house.

Caps for Sale

The picture on the left is the village where the peddler was selling his wares. When the storyboard is opened, to the left is the scene in which the peddler leaves town. On the right is the tree where he fell asleep and the monkeys came and took his caps.

Peter Rabbit

Opening the "fence" reveals the garden drawn inside.

Goldilocks and the Three Bears

Behind the front door of the house, the student has drawn beds, chairs, and bowls of porridge for the three bears.

Sometimes creating the number of puppets needed for the storyboards can be a daunting task in the classroom. For example, if using the story *The Three Billy Goats Gruff,* each student would need four characters: the troll and three billy goats. Let's do the math . . .

Four characters per student times 25 students equals 100 pieces!

Also, some kindergartners take the whole work time just to color and begin cutting out the puppets. My management and organization for these props is that the settings are completed on the bags at school, and puppets go home for homework. Shown are pictures of some puppets from the story *Where the Wild Things Are.*

This activity is a great home-school connection. Students usually make a storyboard each week. Let parents know that on Fridays the storyboards will be going home. Also send home a written summary of the story with the key details that students should include in their retellings. Parents are asked to have their child retell the story using their storyboard props at least two times. Think of all the practice with retelling that kindergartners will have by doing this activity both at school and at home.

Retelling Stroll

This activity asks kindergartners to retell a story as they step on paper rocks and feet to aid their comprehension and retelling. Use the reproducibles of the rock and stepping stone found on pages 83 and 84. Make copies on brown paper, label them like the examples below, and laminate.

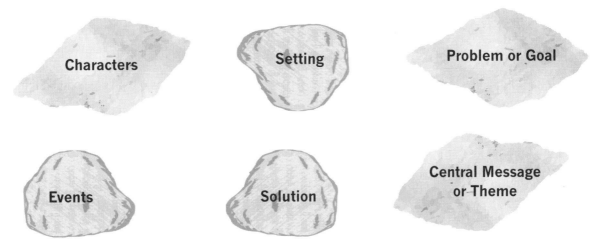

Make several copies of the feet reproducible on page 85 and laminate them. You are now ready to set up a Retelling Stroll. Students will walk on the rocks and feet as they retell a story. When you first begin this activity, organize the stroll so that it represents the story line. This will scaffold students at first.

After you have scaffolded students by giving them the organization for the retelling, the next step is to have them set up their stroll. They can work alone, with a partner, or in a small group. Students will organize their stroll by putting out the appropriate number of feet and rocks.

Let's take a retelling stroll with Juan, a kindergartner, and a Clifford book. In this example, there are two characters, two settings, one problem, one solution, and a theme. The Events rock is not used in this example.

Juan starts his stroll by standing on the Characters rock. He knows there are two characters in the book because there are two feet in front of the Characters rock. As Juan steps onto each foot, he will name a character in the story: first Emily Elizabeth and then Clifford (or vice versa).

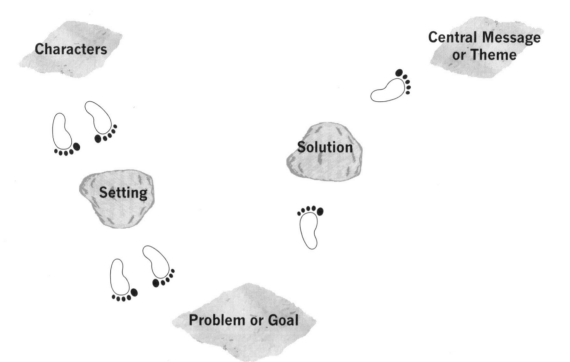

Juan continues his stroll and steps onto the Setting rock. He knows there are two settings in the story because there are two feet in front of the Setting rock. As he steps onto each foot, he will name one of the settings in the story: the park and then Emily Elizabeth's house (or vice versa).

The next rock Juan steps on is Problem or Goal. There is one foot in front of this rock, so there is one problem. Juan tells what the problem is as he steps onto the foot: Emily Elizabeth is planning an outside party for Clifford, but it is going to rain.

Juan now steps onto the Solution rock. There is one foot in front of this rock, so there is one solution: Emily Elizabeth gets a big tent and puts it up in the backyard.

Finally, Juan steps onto the last rock, which is titled Central Message or Theme. He discusses how the theme of friendship was woven throughout the story.

Theme and Central Message

As students are listening to or reading a story, we want them to be aware of what the characters are doing and learning throughout the book. This usually sets the stage for the theme and central message. During or after reading, mark places in the text that lead readers to the theme.

For example, in the children's book titled *Victor*, by Pat Pavelka, Victor the cat moves from the country to the city and is teased by all of the neighborhood cats. At the end of the story the other cats realize what a good friend Victor really is, and they apologize for judging him before getting to know him. The central message in this book could be, "do not judge someone until you get to know them and give them a chance" or "treat others like you would want to be treated." As we reread the story and take a closer look at the actions and reactions of characters, we mark places in the book where the author leads us toward the theme.

Using the reproducible on page 86, write the theme or central message of the story on the lines in the middle of the page. You can write it and then make copies for students or students can copy and write it themselves.

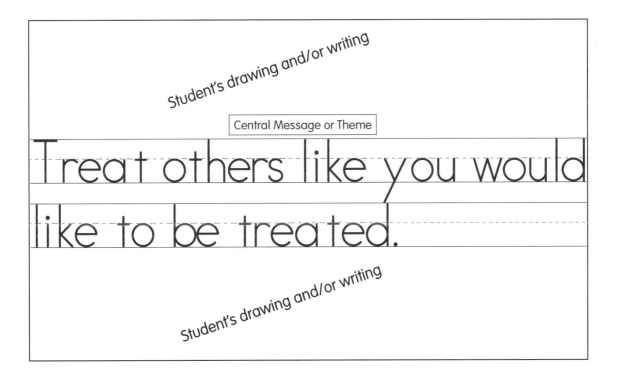

Kindergartners will then draw and/or write about the events, as well as a character's actions and experiences that led them to the theme or central idea.

Event Brochure

Use the reproducibles on pages 87 and 88 to make a brochure that will depict the beginning, middle, and end of a story. The brochure has two reproducibles, one for the front and one for the back. Fold the brochure in thirds. Students draw the beginning, middle, and end of the story.

Beginning

Middle

End

Front

Name

Title

Date

Back

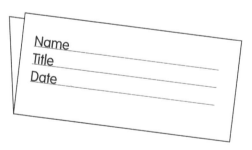

Folded (closed)

Part 1
KEY IDEAS AND DETAILS

Standard 3. *Analyze how and why individuals, events, and ideas develop and interact over the course of a text.*

Kindergarten (RL.K.3)

With prompting and support, identify characters, settings, and major events in a story.

Grade 1 (RL.1.3)

Describe characters, settings, and major events in a story, using key details.

Focusing on meaning throughout the whole story helps students to see how intertwined the characters, settings, and major events are. Students who are carrying meaning throughout the story can make predictions that make sense and are logical. Inferring characters' feelings, motivations, and thoughts then becomes part of students' deeper thinking as they read or listen to a story. We want students to realize and understand that the interactions of these three story parts play a significant role in comprehending explicitly, as well as inferring.

Prediction Monitoring Chart

Remember, students who carry meaning through-out the story can make predictions that are thoughtful and appropriate. Students need to analyze and describe the details in the text that led them to their predictions. They need to cite specific textual evidence! Take a piece of construction paper and fold it into thirds. Label each section as shown in the example.

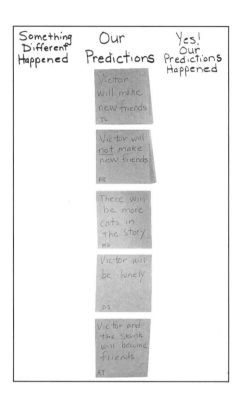

As students make predictions, write their predictions on sticky notes, and put the stickies in the middle section under Our Predictions. As reading continues, students monitor their predictions. Usually one of three things occurs.

The prediction happened.
When a prediction is confirmed in the story, move that sticky from the middle of the chart (Our Predictions) to the right side (Yes! Our Predictions Happened). Students must tell the clues the author gave that helped them make that prediction.

Something different than the prediction happened.
When a prediction does not happen in the story, move that sticky from the middle of the chart to the left side (Something Different Happened). Students must tell why their prediction did not occur and what actually did happen.

Students changed their predictions.

When students want to change their prediction based on something that happened in the text, it shows us they are monitoring comprehension. They are anticipating what is going to happen from one moment to another based on textual support. I use arrows on the stickies to show this. When a prediction has been changed, I draw an arrow on the bottom of the note and move it to the left side (Something Different Happened). The arrow tells me that the student changed his mind based on something that happened in the text. When a new prediction is given, I draw an arrow on the top of the sticky. This tells me that a new prediction was given based on textual support.

In the example below, a student with the initials JL made a prediction that the seeds Frog and Toad planted would grow. The sticky was initially placed in the middle section. As we were reading, the text stated that Frog kept forgetting to water the seeds. JL raised her hand and said, "I change what I thought. The seeds are not going to grow because Frog is not watering them." I put an arrow on the bottom of her original sticky, telling me she changed her mind, and moved it to the left section. I then wrote her new prediction on a sticky with an arrow on the top, showing that she clarified her thoughts based on the text.

These notes are great assessment pieces. I put them in my anecdotal records notebook. You will be able to see trends very quickly. For some students, arrows are always a part of their stickies because they are able to anticipate what will happen next. These are students who are monitoring their comprehension and can carry meaning from page to page. Other students make predictions that rarely come true. When I put their stickies in my anecdotal notebook, I put a minus on the bottom to show me the prediction did not come true.

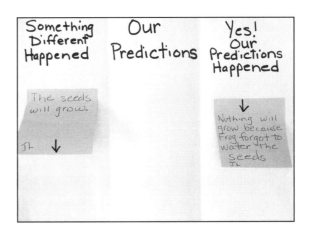

Story Element Booklets

At the very basic level, kindergartners are required to identify characters, setting, and major events in a story. Using the reproducibles on pages 89 and 90, students can make story element booklets.

The title of the book is

The author is

The illustrator is

My name is

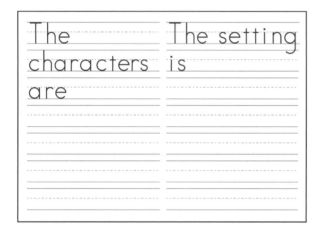

In addition to their drawings, students are asked to write the names of characters and the setting.

The events may be more complicated for students, and there may be several key events to consider. Therefore, on this event page, students are asked only to illustrate. No writing is needed.

Major events are

Character Discussion Cards

When asking kindergartners to retell familiar stories, we are also looking for them to include some very specific things such as characters, settings, events, problems and solutions, and endings. As they include these story elements, the goal is to have students go to a deeper level in their discussions.

Copy the reproducible on page 91 onto heavy stock. Cut the eight items apart to make cards to help students elaborate as they talk about characters in books. Spread the cards out on the floor. Have students choose different cards and describe those aspects of the character.

Character's name	What does the character look like?
What does the character like?	What does the character dislike?
What is the character's problem?	What does the character do to solve the problem?
Describe the character's personality.	Would you like the character as your friend? Explain.

Character Class Books

These cards can also be used for independent assignments. As students become familiar with these character discussion cards, they can use them as a basis for making class character books. After reading a story, pass out the cards to students and have each child draw and/or write about the character based on the card they received. Put all of their pages together to create a class book describing a character in detail. Put these class books in your reading center for the year. Students love going back to these books day after day. The books also help students remember characters that they read about months ago.

Individual Character Books

This is the same activity as described above with Character Class Books, except students make their own books using at least four of the character discussion cards for ideas. Students' individual books are at least four pages in length.

Setting Discussion Cards

When asking kindergartners to retell familiar stories, we are also looking for them to include some very specific things such as characters, settings, events, problems and solutions, and endings. As they include these story elements, the goal is to have students go to a deeper level in their discussions.

Copy the reproducible on page 92 onto heavy stock. Cut the eight items apart to make cards to help students elaborate as they talk about settings in books. Spread the cards out on the floor. Have students choose different cards and describe those aspects of the setting.

Place	Season
Time	See
Hear	Smell
Touch	Taste

Setting Class Books

These cards can also be used as independent assignments. As students become familiar with these setting discussion cards, they can use them as a basis for making class books. After reading a story, pass out the cards to students and have each child draw and/or write about the setting based on the card they received. Put all of their pages together to create a class book describing a setting in detail. Put these class books in your reading center for the year. Students love going back to these books day after day. The books also help students remember settings that they read about months ago.

Individual Setting Books

This is the same activity as described above with Setting Class Books, except students make their own books using at least four of the setting discussion cards for ideas. Students' individual books are at least four pages in length.

Agree/Disagree

Using the reproducible on page 93, give students a statement to either defend or reject. In the example below, students were given the statement: Farfallina and Marcel are good friends. First kindergartners copy the statement onto their papers. Next, they circle "Yes! I agree" on the left side of the page or "No! I disagree" on the right side. Finally, they draw and/or write to back up their opinion based on the text.

The examples below were completed by two kindergartners after reading the book *Farfallina & Marcel* by Holly Keller.

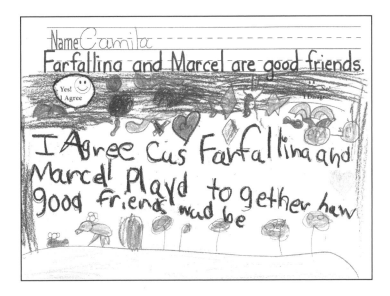

CRAFT AND STRUCTURE

Anchor Standards 4–6

RL.K.4–6

This category of Craft and Structure requires students to look at how a text is written. Students need to understand how the author's choice of words, language, point of view, and style affect the reader's comprehension of the story. Here students' attention focuses on craft, structure, and language.

Part 2
CRAFT AND STRUCTURE

Standard 4. *Interpret words and phrases as they are used in a text, including determining technical, connotative, and figurative meanings, and analyze how specific word choices shape meaning or tone.*

Kindergarten (RL.K.4)

Ask and answer questions about unknown words in a text.

Grade 1 (RL.1.4)

Identify words and phrases in stories or poems that suggest feelings or appeal to the senses.

This standard is asking readers to pay attention to word choice and language. Vocabulary plays an important part in students' reading development. Biemiller states that "Vocabulary size is predictive of later reading achievement."

When working with unknown words, write them on index cards so they can be used for many of the different activities explained in this section.

Read-alouds are excellent resources to use to build expertise in this area.

Hayes and Ahrens have stated that children's books have more rare words per hundred than are typically heard in conversations between college-educated adults.

Treasure Box of Stories and Words

In order for students to begin using rich vocabulary in their daily speaking and writing, they need to be repeatedly exposed to these words. Students will not apply and utilize words they have heard only once. This activity savors a read-aloud book all year as students revisit its vocabulary and use those words in conversation.

This treasure box was found at a craft store. Students decorated it with glitter, markers, stickers, etc.

In the box are plastic bags for read-alouds. Each bag contains an item, or items, that symbolizes and/or represents something from the story, as well as index cards with vocabulary from the story. Following are some photos from sample plastic bags.

The Very Hungry Caterpillar   *Chicka Chicka Boom Boom*

If You Give a Mouse a Cookie   *If You Take a Mouse to School*

Shown are index cards with the vocabulary words from the book *Chrysanthemum* by Kevin Henkes. These cards, as well as three mice, a chrysanthemum flower, a school bus, and some plastic music notes were placed into the baggie after reading the story.

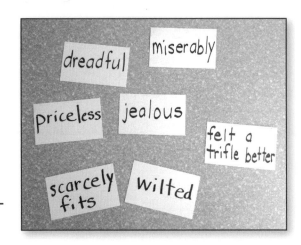

Take out objects and talk about their significance in the story. Have students give a retelling of the story. Review all of the vocabulary words and phrases. The goal is to have students make connections to these words and phrases. For example, the following questions ask students to internalize and make connections with the words and phrases from this story.

> *What would make you feel a trifle better?*
> *What might have happened if you needed something to make you feel a trifle better?*
>
> *Tell me something dreadful!*
> *When would you feel dreadful?*

Ask students to finish the following sentences.
> *I feel jealous when . . .*
> *Something that is priceless is . . .*
>
> *Have you ever tried on something that scarcely fits?*
> *What would scarcely fit into your lunchbox?*
> *What would scarcely fit in the palm of your hand?*

Provide students with scenarios and ask them to decide whether or not each scenario would be priceless or dreadful. Students must explain their answers.

Look at word choice. Why did the author choose "felt a trifle better" instead of "felt just great"? Why did the author choose to say "scarcely fits" instead of "doesn't fit at all"?

Prompts

As students are exposed to new words and begin building their vocabularies, we want to give them the tools and strategies needed to figure out and comprehend these new words and phrases. The following prompts help students begin to internalize how unknown words and phrases can be figured out by thinking about what is happening in the text.

> I heard the word _____. I think it means _____ because _____.
>
> The author used the word _____ instead of _____ because _____.

Shower Liner Grid

This activity allows students to work with vocabulary words and make connections, categorize words, or just practice using them in conversation. Take a shower curtain liner. Divide the liner into sections using colored masking or electrical tape. Following are different ways to use the shower liner grid.

Categorizing Words

After reading a story, brainstorm as many words and phrases as possible that are related to the story. For example, when we finished reading *Goldilocks and the Three Bears*, my kindergartners came up with the following list:

Goldilocks, girl, Mama Bear, Papa Bear, Baby Bear, porridge, woods, eating, rocking, sleeping, small, medium, large, knock, door, run, bold, scared, someone's been . . . , just right, too . . .

I wrote these words on index cards and laid them on the floor. Students took turns choosing cards and making a graph showing how the words are related.

Roll a Cube

In each box of the grid, put an index card with a vocabulary word. Students take turns choosing a card from the grid and then using the cube reproducible found on page 94. They roll the cube and apply what they rolled.

VOCABULARY CUBE

Synonym—The student gives a synonym for the vocabulary word.

Antonym—The student says an antonym for the vocabulary word.

Definition—The student gives a definition of the vocabulary word. The student gives the meaning in his/her own words.

Sentence—The word is used in a sentence by the student. The sentence must be about home, school, or the student. This stops students from repeating the sentence from the story.

Connect to you—The student tells how the word is connected to his/her life. For example, if the word is "scrawny," a connection might be: "When I first got my dog from the pound, she was scrawny. Now she has gained weight and her fur is shiny."

Importance to the story—The student discusses why that word is important to the story and why that particular word might have been used instead of another word. Students talk about the subtleties of the word that was used. For example: "blustery" instead of "cold."

My students often want to take the cards from the baggies in the treasure box and use them on the grid. When choosing a word, we can now discuss what story the word came from and decide whether or not it could be used in another story. If yes, why? If no, then why not? For example, students decided that the word "scrawny" could not be used in our Clifford book because Clifford is not scrawny, nor is any character in the book scrawny.

Part 2
CRAFT AND STRUCTURE

Standard 5. *Analyze the structure of texts, including how specific sentences, paragraphs, and larger portions of the text (e.g., a section, chapter, scene, or stanza) relate to each other and the whole.*

Kindergarten (RL.K.5)

Recognize common types of texts (e.g., storybooks, poems).

Grade 1 (RL.1.5)

Explain major differences between books that tell stories and books that give information, drawing on a wide reading of a range of text types.

The goal of this standard is to use text structure to increase comprehension of texts. Students need to be able to analyze and discuss the different types of features present in different kinds of texts such as stories, poems, plays, and nonfiction.

Book Sorts

Provide students with a tub of books. Have four to five books available in each of the following categories: stories, poems, plays, and nonfiction. Use the shower liner grid described on page 35 to categorize the books. Students take turns choosing a book and deciding where it should be placed on the grid. They must give at least two reasons for why they are placing it in a certain category.

Personal Poetry Books

The more exposure and practice students have with text structures, the more they can begin to internalize these organizations and use them to increase comprehension. Poetry has some very specific structural elements. Knowing these elements, the way the author has organized the text, will help students synthesize information as poetry is read. There are several elements that make up a poem. Elements relating to poetry that kindergartners should be exposed to include, but are not limited to:

Rhythm: *This is the "music" or beat of the poem made by the stressed and unstressed syllables.*

Stanza: *Stanzas are a series of lines grouped together and separated from other stanzas by an empty line.*

Rhyme: *If a poem has rhyme, the last words of the lines sound alike.*

These elements of poetry are some of the basic essential parts of the structure of a poem. However, this does not mean that all poems must have all these elements.

Have your students create poetry books using spiral notebooks or composition books. Each week give students a poem to cut, color, and glue into their poetry books. Refer to the different elements of the poem. Compare and contrast the different poems each week. Reread the poems and look for connections among them with regard to the elements or meaning. Rereading the poems throughout the year also increases fluency and allows for close reading. Below are some examples of poetry notebooks.

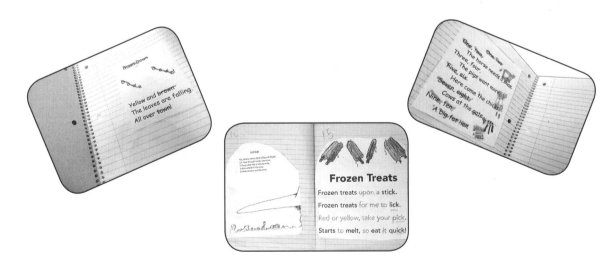

Character Headbands

Drama is text that presents a story told entirely in dialogue and action. It is written with the intent of being acted out. Like poems, drama and plays have some very specific structural elements. Knowing these elements, the way the author has organized the text, will help students synthesize information as plays are read and acted out. Elements relating to drama that kindergartners should be exposed to include, but are not limited to:

Characters: *Usually they are given as a list at the beginning of the play.*

Scenes: *The setting.*

Dialogue: *The words spoken by the characters in the play.*

Props: *The items characters need. They are usually given as a list at the beginning of different scenes.*

Character headbands are very simple resources to use when putting on a play in the kindergarten classroom. The examples to the right are from the plays *The Little Red Hen* and *Goldilocks and the Three Bears*. A picture of the character is attached to a sentence strip. The sentence strip is then stapled, making a headband for a student to wear. With this easy process, students are exposed to and act out plays a number of times each month.

Semantic Feature Analysis

Semantic feature analysis is an excellent tool to use with kindergartners as we study the differences between stories, poems, plays/drama, and nonfiction texts. Semantic mapping and semantic feature analysis encourage students to be critical thinkers. They help demonstrate the relationships among concepts and different categories (Pittelman). Roll out butcher paper and make the following chart.

	Storybook	Poem	Play	Nonfiction
Rhythm				
Stanza				
Rhyme				
List of Characters				
Scenes				
Dialogue				
Props				
Title				
Author				
Illustrator/Illustrations				
Tells a Story				
Table of Contents				
Headings				
Captions				
Facts				
Diagrams				

Use butcher paper so this can be rolled up and taken out easily as you work with different texts. Give students colored chips to put in the appropriate boxes as you read and analyze different texts.

CRAFT AND STRUCTURE

Standard 6. *Assess how point of view or purpose shapes the content and style of a text.*

Kindergarten (RL.K.6)
With prompting and support, name the author and illustrator of a story and define the role of each in telling the story.

Grade 1 (RL.1.6)
Identify who is telling the story at various points in a text.

The Craft and Structure standards focus on how the text is being presented. As students converse daily about author, illustrator, and point of view, they internalize how these concepts play a key role in reading for meaning. Kindergartners should be able to have conversations about how the styles of authors and illustrators affect comprehension.

Illustration Conversation Chart

Make and display the following chart.

How do the illustrations . . .

* show characters' feelings and emotions?
* show what the character is thinking?
* show problem and solution?
* show setting?
* show events?
* help create the mood of the text?

As you or your students are reading a text, discuss the items listed on the chart. Be sure to work with each of the four text structures from RL.K.5: stories, poems, plays, and non-fiction. Put sticky notes on the exact places in the illustrations that depict concepts from the chart. The more you analyze and closely read illustrations, the more you will add to this chart. As students discuss the pictures, they will begin to see how much information the illustrations provide about the text.

How Did You Tell Us?

In this activity students are asked to think about how both illustrations and text tell the story.

In reading the text below, we know Victor is not happy because the text states:

"I am not happy here in the country"

"Victor sighed"

"Why won't anyone be my friend?"

"I am not happy here in the country," Victor sighed. "Why won't anyone be my friend?"

15

In looking at the illustration on this page, we see the same thing. Victor is lying on the branch alone. He has a sad face. There are three kittens in the background that are having a good time with no regard to Victor, who is alone on the branch.

Kindergartners can start to draw conclusions about the three kittens just from the text and the illustration on this page. The text states, "Why won't anyone be my friend?" It implies that Victor has tried to make friends, and no one would be his friend. The three kittens in the illustration are playing close enough to see Victor, yet he is not included.

Use the reproducible on page 95 to give students a statement, and then have them explain how the author and illustrator "told" this in the story. In the example to the right, students are given the statement: How did you tell us the kittens were mean to Victor? Kindergartners would then show how the illustrator depicted this on the page and what words the author used to prove it.

Name

Title

How did you tell us the kittens were mean to Victor?

Illustrator

Author

Matching Illustrations with Text

As students are working with texts, we want them to see that the illustrator is telling the same story that the author is telling. In defining the roles of each, we discuss how the author uses print while the illustrator uses pictures.

The following prompts help students see how the roles of both author and illustrator are interconnected.

When the author wrote _____, the illustrator showed this by _____.

When the illustrator showed _____, the author actually said _____.

Use the reproducibles on pages 96 and 97 to have students practice and show their understanding of the roles of author and illustrator.

Name
Title
The illustrator drew

The author wrote

Name
Title
The author wrote

The illustrator showed
this by drawing

Wordless Books

Wordless books are excellent resources to model the important role illustrators have in telling a story. Wordless books are books that contain illustrations and no text. They model story structure such as characters, settings, events, problem, and solution all through the illustrations. Have students talk about what an author could write for each illustration. We want students to practice close reading of the illustrations, not just the text.

A center I always have available for students is a wordless-book center. Students become the authors for wordless books. Some students just label things they see in the pictures, while others are writing stories based on the pictures.

Form three to four different heterogeneous groups with your students. Have the different groups each become the authors of a wordless book. After each group has dictated their stories, work with comparing and contrasting the different stories. Graph the similarities and differences using Venn diagrams or T-charts.

I had a wealth of wordless books in my classroom that students were not really using, until I made the books manipulative and guided students a bit more. If you have access to a laminator, rip the books apart and send each page through the laminator—yes, it is hard to rip a book apart, but after the first tear it gets easier! If you do not have a laminator, notebook sheet protectors will also work.

Put all of the laminated pages of the wordless book into a large manila envelope or bin. Have students take the pictures and put them in correct order of the story. I hear them talking the stories through and pretending they are the authors. This supports students practicing close reading of the illustrations, not just the text.

Following is a list of wordless books your kindegartners might enjoy.

Title	Author
A Boy, a Dog, and a Frog	Mercer Mayer
A Boy, a Dog, a Frog, and a Friend	Mercer Mayer
Changes, Changes	Pat Hutchins
Deep in the Forest	Brinton Turkle
Dinosaur Day	Liza Donnelly
Flotsam	David Wiesner
Flowers for the Snowman	Gerda Marie Scheidl and Jozef Wildon
Free Fall	David Wiesner
Frog on His Own	Mercer Mayer
Frog, Where Are You?	Mercer Mayer
Good Dog, Carl (series)	Alexandra Day
Oops	Arthur Geisert
Oink	Arthur Geisert
Pancakes for Breakfast	Tomie DePaola
Picnic	Emily McCully
Rain	Peter Spier
The Chicken's Child	Margaret Hartelius
The Grey Lady and the Strawberry Snatcher	Molly Bang
The Mysteries of Harris Burdick	Chris Van Allsburg
The Red Book	Barbara Lehman
The Snowman	Raymond Briggs
We Hide, You Seek	Jose Aruego and Ariane Dewey
Will's Mammoth	Rafe Martin and Stephen Gammell
You Can't Take a Balloon Into The Museum of Fine Arts	Jacqueline Preiss Weitzman
Zoom	Istvan Banyai

Point of View

Basically, stories are usually written from a first person or third person point of view.

First person: One of the characters is telling the story.
Third Person: The author is narrating the story.

As students are deciding who is telling the story, we need to go back into the text and prove their ideas. Reread the text and look for point-of-view clues. Put sticky notes on places in the text that support a specific point of view.

Write the following on chart paper and prominently display it near your read-aloud area.

Who is telling the story?

How would the story be different if it were told from another point of view?

How would the story be different if it were told from your own point of view?

Integration of Knowledge and Ideas

Anchor Standards 7 and 9
RL.K.7 and 9

This category of Integration of Knowledge and Ideas

requires that students be able to evaluate how an

illustrator has depicted a scene, character, setting, item,

etc., described by the author. Students need to focus

on how the illustrator and author both address charac-

ters, settings, and events within texts.

INTEGRATION OF KNOWLEDGE AND IDEAS

Standard 7. *Integrate and evaluate content presented in diverse media and formats, including visually and quantitatively, as well as in words.*

Kindergarten (RL.K.7)

With prompting and support, describe the relationship between illustrations and the story in which they appear (e.g., what moment in a story an illustration depicts).

Grade 1 (RL.1.7)

Use illustrations and details in a story to describe its characters, setting, or events.

Students need to notice and use all of the different things that give books meaning, not just the words. This includes illustrations, photos, and speech bubbles, as well as sound and video. Picture walks are an integral part of guided reading lessons because of the meaning that is carried in the illustrations and the relationship between author and illustrator.

Prompts

Chart these prompts and questions and prominently display them in your classroom. As you work with author and illustrator relationships, use these as discussion starters.

The author most likely included this to show _____.

The illustrator most likely included this to show _____.

Did the illustration capture what the text says? Why? Why not?

How does the illustration connect with the author's words?

How does the illustration help you understand what the author wrote?

Cover and Predict

Text to Illustration
Cover the illustrations in a book. After reading a page, stop and brainstorm all of the things you would expect to find in the illustration. Ask students to tell you how they got that picture in their heads. What words did the author use that helped them make a movie in their heads? What words helped them visualize the text? Kindergartners are required to describe the relationship between illustrations and the story. We want them to be able to converse about what moment in the story the illustration depicts.

Illustration to Text
Follow the same procedure as above, but this time cover the text. After studying an illustration, stop and brainstorm all of the things you would expect to find in the text. Kindergartners are required to describe the relationship between illustrations and the text. We want them to be able to converse about what words in the story support the illustration.

Text and Illustration Connections

Reading the Illustrations Only
This is different from Cover and Predict because here the whole book is being read, rather than stopping and thinking after each page as in the activity above. Read the story using only the illustrations. Students must use only the support from the pictures to comprehend the story. Note things about characters, setting, events, problem, and solution.

Reading the Text Only
Read the story using only the text. Do not show the pictures. Students must use only the support from the text to comprehend the story. Note things about characters, setting, events, problem, and solution.

Compare and contrast these two readings. Which was easier for students: reading the text without the pictures or reading the pictures without the text? Discuss how powerful it is when readers rely on the relationship of both text and illustrations.

Character Interpretations

Use the reproducibles on pages 98 and 101 to show the relationship between text and illustrations with regard to a character.

Folded in half

Opened

Setting Interpretations

Use the reproducibles on pages 99 and 101 to show the relationship between text and illustrations with regard to a setting.

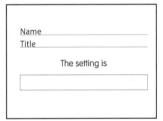

Folded in half

Opened

Event Interpretations

Use the reproducibles on pages 100 and 101 to show the relationship between text and illustrations with regard to an event.

Folded in half

Opened

Title and Cover Connections

Below are questions that begin conversations about text and illustration relationships.

Based on the title, what illustrations do you expect to see?

Based on the cover picture, what words and phrases do you expect to read?

Based on the title and cover, what do you already know about characters? Setting? Events?

Favorite Parts

Favorite Part of the Text
Have students choose a favorite part of the story based on the text. What did the author write that they really liked? Use the reproducible on page 102 to have students record their thoughts.

Name
Title
My favorite part of the story is
_____
_____
_____
(Picture)

Name
Title
My favorite illustration is
_____
_____
_____
(Picture)

Favorite Illustration
Have students choose a favorite illustration in the book. Use the reproducible on page 103 to have them record their thoughts.

Part 3
INTEGRATION OF KNOWLEDGE AND IDEAS

Standard 9. *Analyze how two or more texts address similar themes or topics in order to build knowledge or to compare the approaches the authors take.*

Kindergarten (RL.K.9)

With prompting and support, compare and contrast the adventures and experiences of characters in familiar stories.

Grade 1 (RL.1.9)

Compare and contrast the adventures and experiences of characters in stories.

This anchor standard requires that students be able to carry meaning across different texts. Important is the ability to compare and contrast, make connections, and see themes and central ideas intertwined among different texts.

Comparing and Contrasting

Characters
Chart the following to use as the starting point for discussions.

Compare and contrast characters with regard to their:

Likes   Dislikes

Strengths   Weaknesses

Home Lives   School Lives

Friendships   Problems and Solutions

Reactions to Problems   Physical Appearances

Personalities   Adventures

Experiences

Stories in General

There are many different elements and concepts to compare and contrast from text to text. Chart the following to use as the starting point for discussions.

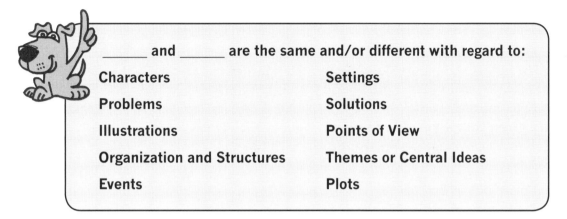

_____ and _____ are the same and/or different with regard to:

Characters	Settings
Problems	Solutions
Illustrations	Points of View
Organization and Structures	Themes or Central Ideas
Events	Plots

Notice that all of the above items are a part of standards 1 through 10. Venn diagrams and T-charts work well with this chart.

Character Pictures

Character Pictures is an activity that can be done weekly to compare and contrast different characters from different texts. This is one of my students' favorite activities. Instead of giving students a character to use for this activity, provide them with part of a character. For example, cut the character in half lengthwise or horizontally and give them a part; or give them just the character's head or body. Students take the part of the character, glue it onto a piece of paper, and turn it into a picture. The pictures must be about something that happened in the book. Some suggestions are:

Character's Experiences

Adventure the Character Had

Problem the Character Faced

Solution to the Problem

Major Event Involving the Character

These two pictures are based on the book *More Spaghetti I Say.* Kindergartners were given yellow yarn to represent spaghetti. They drew pictures of what Minnie and Freddy did with the spaghetti.

This picture was done after reading *Owl Moon.*

This picture was done after reading a book about Clifford.

Character Wall

Each week, one or two students donate their pictures to be hung up on the Character Wall. This is a place where at least one character a week is displayed. As new texts are being read, students are constantly looking at this wall to make connections between characters from different stories. Kindergartners are now comparing and contrasting the adventures and experiences of characters on a daily basis.

Character Photo Book

This activity is the same as above except instead of having a Character Wall, students are using an actual photo book to store the pictures.

Prompts

Characters
How is _____ like _____?

How is Frog like Toad?

How is Junie B. Jones like Emily Elizabeth?

How is Goldilocks like the Troll?

Which character would you rather have as a friend?

Which character in this book would get along well with a character in another book? Why?

Which character in this book would not get along well with a character in another book? Why not?

What recommendation would a character in the story _____ make to a character in the story _____?

Who does _____ remind you of? Why?

Author and Illustrator
How is an author like an illustrator?

How is an illustrator like an author?

Analogies
Clifford is to Emily Elizabeth as Frog is to _____.
   (Toad)

The house is to *Goldilocks and the Three Bears* as the bridge is to _____.
   (The Three Billy Goats Gruff)

The crumbs are to Hansel and Gretel as the Yellow Brick Road is to _____.
   (Dorothy)

Range of Reading and Level of Text Complexity
Anchor Standard 10
RL.K.10

This category requires that students be able to read and comprehend many types of narrative and informational texts. Some examples include stories, poems, plays, how-to texts, and magazine articles. It is important for students to progress toward being able to read complex grade-level texts with appropriate fluency, comprehension, and metacognitive strategies.

Part 4
RANGE OF READING AND LEVEL OF TEXT COMPLEXITY

Standard 10. *Read and comprehend complex literary and informational texts independently and proficiently.*

Kindergarten (RL.K.10)

Actively engage in group reading activities with purpose and understanding.

Grade 1 (RL.1.10)

With prompting and support, read prose and poetry of appropriate complexity for grade 1.

It is recognized that an important goal for students is to be able to read grade-level texts. At the heart of reading these grade-level texts is the ability to handle the comprehension of them in a deeper, more thought-provoking manner. All of the activities in this book allow students to be actively engaged in group-reading activities with purpose and understanding. It is during shared reading with big books and read-aloud times that students are working with standards 1 through 9, utilizing the activities and then follow-up assignments.

Students are required to handle complex pieces of literature as well as nonfiction. In order to achieve this, students must be reading extensively and have access to texts that can be read with success.

One of the first goals we have for young children is for them to know that reading is life! Reading is all around us in almost everything we do. There are two different types of reading materials students are involved with in the kindergarten classroom. One is a personal reading box. The other is the classroom reading center or library.

Reading Boxes

Using reading boxes ensures that students are involved with reading texts they can successfully read accurately and with ease. "Reading is a message-getting, problem-solving activity that increases in fluency and flexibility every time it is practiced correctly" writes Dr. Marie Clay. Students need to be involved with materials at their independent levels. Richard Alllington says, "You can't learn much from books you can't read." The goal of organizing reading boxes is to have them matched as closely as possible to students' reading levels so they can practice reading with meaning.

We want our students reading. That is the ultimate goal. Because kindergartners are often "flippers," just flipping through pages and saying, "I'm done," we need to turn their attention to the print and pictures. The reading box is full of many items that are not books. Again, books are the ultimate goal, but for some children just getting them to read a cereal box or the name of a friend is a monumental step.

Familiarity with books allows students to be independent and easily apply, practice, and utilize reading strategies.

Reading Box Contents

When boxes are initially created, they are filled with familiar, old favorite reading materials. The following items have been used successfully in reading boxes.

Class Lists
Students are so excited to read each others' names. Make a list of names of students in your class. Put pictures of classmates next to their names to help with the reading.

School Lists
The class lists were so successful that we created school lists in the reading boxes. School lists are names of any people who are associated with the school. Your list may include the principal, the secretary, teachers, custodians, cooks, crossing guards, bus drivers, etc. Put pictures next to the names, if possible.

Box Books
Box books are great ways to use environmental print. Have students bring in cereal or similar boxes. Cut off the tops and bottoms of the boxes. The boxes will now fold down flat. Put three to five boxes together, punch two holes, and tie them together with yarn or use chicken rings to put them together into a box book.

Book Covers
Many hardcover books have book jackets on them. Remove the jackets from the books. Put three or four book jackets together, punch holes, and tie the jackets with yarn.

Wordless Books
The students' language development increases as they tell stories about the wordless books. They work with the concepts of beginning, middle, and end, as well as story elements. These books help students attend to pictures.

Books
Two requirements need to be met by books before they can be placed in reading boxes. First, they need to be familiar to the students. Students must have worked with or heard the story at least one time. Second, the books need to be at students' independent reading levels. Leveled readers are great to use.

Poems
Seasonal poems are fun for students to read over and over again.

Pledge of Allegiance
Listen to your students recite the pledge. Many of them really do not know what the words are. Make copies of the Pledge of Allegiance and add them to reading boxes.

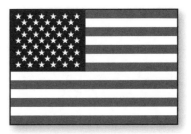

Charts and Chants from Around Your Room
Anything that is displayed in your room can be copied or typed and put in the box. I found that my students often read the things on the wall only when I took the items over to them and we did some choral and shared reading. Now that the items are in book boxes, students are reading those things many times on their own. I have seen a lot of improvement in whole-class reading of chants and charts because students are practicing them more!

Menus
On Fridays, when menus are passed out at school for the following week, they are also put into the reading boxes.

Bag Books
Paper bags are great sources of environmental print. Bring in bags from different stores and restaurants. Put three to five bags together, punch holes, and tie them together with yarn to make a "bag book."

Notices
Any appropriate notice that is sent home can be placed into the boxes.

Baseball Cards
Any sports cards (baseball, football, or basketball) are great to use.

Calendar Area
Think about your calendar area. There is a wealth of reading available there: days of the week, months of the year, holidays, birthdays, seasons.

Vocabulary Words from Science and Social Studies Curricula
Add your vocabulary words to the boxes to give students extra practice time.

Guided Reading Group Materials
Materials in the reading box can be directly coordinated with those used by your guided reading groups.

Reading Center/Classroom Library

Variety of Materials
In our reading centers or libraries, we need to ensure that students have a wealth of texts available that they are interested in and excited about. A repertoire of text types should be available, including, but not limited to:

Magazines	*Poems*
Picture Books	*Graphic Novels*
Novels/Chapter Books	*Comic Books*
Research Books	*Textbooks*

Mini Posters
As we work with different areas of the Common Core, students are expected to apply and utilize the strategies taught. Some kindergartners will be able to visit the reading center and immediately internalize and apply the reading strategies discussed. Others will need support in order to practice what is being taught. That's where mini posters come in.

As you work with each standard, have students help you write directions to, and reminders for, applying and utilizing the strategies introduced for the standard. Put these on mini posters, made from 12 x 18-inch construction paper. You can make these posters as simple or integrated as you need. Make a mini poster with students after working with identifying characters, settings, and the major events in the story through illustrations (RL.K.3).

1. **Enjoy your book!**

2. **Place your** ▢ **on all the pages where you can find the character.**

3. **Place your** ▢ **on all the pages where you can find the setting.**

4. **Place your** ◇ **on all the pages where you can find the major events that have taken place.**

I have three things available for students to use to mark and post on the books: stickies, wikki stix, and highlighting tape. After students mark and post in their books, they must share their postings with a friend before they can remove them from the book.

Use the information below to make a mini poster with students after working with standard RL.K.1.

Ask questions as you read!

I wonder who . . . ?

I wonder what . . . ?

I wonder where . . . ?

I wonder why . . . ?

I wonder when . . . ?

I wonder how . . . ?

Home and School Connections

As educators, we understand that learning to read is a significant achievement for our young children. When home-school partnerships exist, we create powerful supports that encourage students to become life-long, strategic readers. Unfortunately for many children, the kindergarten classroom is the first real exposure they have to print and books. It would behoove us to create partnerships in which students are being read to at home, as well as taking materials home to read themselves. Below are three fun activities parents can do with their children at home and outside of school.

"The best way to raise a reader is to read to that child in the home and in the classroom." *Jim Trelease*

Reading Aloud Every Day
Reading aloud is one of the most important ways parents can spend time with their children.

Reading House Blueprint
Children need to see that some kind of reading can be found in almost every room of their homes. Brainstorm a list with your students of rooms in their homes (kitchen, bedroom, bathroom, garage, living room, dining room, etc.). Have each student make a blueprint or map of his house to take home. Have parents and their children try to find examples of all the places where reading materials are found in those rooms. Students can draw and/or write all the items found on their blueprints or maps.

"Children who come from homes in which storybook reading takes place have an educational advantage over those who do not." *Strickland & Morrow*

Reading Scavenger Hunt
Children need to see that reading is also found in every aspect of life. Brainstorm a list with your students of all the places outside of their houses that they visit each week or month (neighbor's house, friend's house, school, public library, grocery store, gas station, drug store, shopping mall, stores, etc.). Have parents and their children try to find examples of reading in all of those places they visit. Students can draw and/or write about their findings.

Assessment

Assessment must drive instruction, not be seen as just a completion of instruction. And if assessment drives instruction, then we need to assess before and especially during instruction, not just after. Teacher observation is the center of ongoing assessment and evaluation. We are constantly collecting and gathering information. We then use that information to guide our instruction, form flexible groups, and create follow-up assignments.

Assessment

Assessment is a forever, on-going process for educators. As students engage in whole- and small-group learning situations and work through assignments, we must continually assess their progress. The visual below follows the cyclical path of assessment, evaluation, and instruction.

Assessment
First, we collect information. We watch and observe what happens in whole groups and in small-group settings. We look at the work that is being completed during assignment times and at centers.

On-Going and Continuous

Evaluation
Next, we analyze the collected information. We look for strengths and weaknesses. We see concepts that have been mastered or need improvement. **And** we group or regroup because **evaluation drives instruction.**

Instruction
Then, we implement specific, research-based instructional strategies to help students master the standards and concepts. **Lastly**, we repeat the process again and again and again!

Whole-Group Assessments

In kindergarten, much of our instruction is done in a whole-group setting. The formative assessments described here are designed to be used in whole-group settings. They are a process that is used on a daily basis, not a specific test. They happen before, during, and after instruction.

When working in a whole-class setting, it is a daunting task to think about continually assessing all students. The goal of the following strategies is for you to be able to easily note and document students' learning. My biggest requirement for these daily assessments is that *they must be manageable for us*!

Envelope Response Puppets

Usually, when I want my whole class to answer a question, I ask them to give me a thumbs-up or thumbs-down. It is often difficult to assess their responses. Some students have their thumbs sideways; some are just looking at their neighbor and making the same motion; and others give a thumbs-up or -down for a quick second and are done. This activity lets students make a decision and "holds" that decision for you to observe. I use this activity for just about all of the standards.

Take a white letter-sized envelope, seal it up, and then cut it in half. You have just made two response puppets!

Yes or No?

Take one half of each envelope and write "yes" on one side and "no" on the other. As you ask questions, students hold up the corresponding side to answer them.

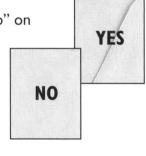

Below are specific examples from different texts.

RL.K.1 Goldilocks knocked on the door before she went into the Bears' house.

RL.K.2 After Goldilocks ate Baby Bear's porridge, she went into the bedroom and fell asleep.

RL.K.3 The setting for *Frog and Toad Together* is outside in the garden.

RL.K.4 Brave is a synonym for the word "bold."

RL.K.5 *The Little Red Hen* is a poem.

RL.K.6 Jan Brett is the author of the book *The Mitten*.

RL.K.7 The picture on page _____ does a good job of illustrating the author's words.

RL.K.9 Frog and Toad have a friendship like Emily Elizabeth and Clifford.

Don't stop after getting the "yes" or "no" responses. These responses are the beginning for deeper conversations and understanding. Ask the students who answered "yes" to tell you why. For students who answered "no," ask them to explain why not.

Smiles or Frowns?

Take the other half of the envelopes and make a happy face on one side and a sad face on the other. As you ask questions, students hold up the corresponding side to answer them.

Below are general ideas for questions.

RL.K.1 Ask any question about a specific text.

RL.K.2 Retell part of a story, and ask if it is in the correct order.

RL.K.3 The setting for _____ is _____.

RL.K.4 _____ is a synonym for _____.

RL.K.5 _____ is a poem.

RL.K.6 _____ is the author of the book _____.

RL.K.7 The author and illustrator told the same event on page _____ in different ways.

RL.K.9 _____ is like _____.

Remember to ask students to explain their thinking. Why did they hold up the smile and not the frown or vice versa?

Class List Stickies with Posterboard

This is a strategy that has two goals. The first is that it helps ensure we ask all of our students to be active participants in conversations and learning. The second goal of this strategy is to monitor progress as we are working with our whole class.

Encouraging Active Participation

Put each student's name on a separate sticky note, and place these stickies on a piece of posterboard. Write their names so the sticky part is on the bottom. (You will understand why when you read the next activity.)

As you are asking questions and having conversations about texts, pull students' names off the posterboard as they participate. When all of the stickies have been removed, that shows that all students have had at least one turn to participate.

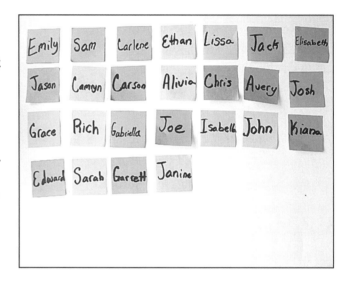

There is one management idea that makes a difference in how successful this activity is. Once students have their names removed from the chart, we do not want them to feel they are "done!" So after every third or fourth student's name gets taken off the chart, pull a name from the pile that has already been removed. We want students to know that you will be choosing names from the chart, as well as names that have already been pulled off. This keeps their attention, whether or not their name has been taken off.

Monitoring Progress Using Paper Plate Rubrics

There are many assessments we give to students individually, recording their responses as a "test" or end-of-lesson grade. However, the formative assessments shown here are used on a daily basis and are more general. For example, Standard RL.K.2 states, "With prompting and support, retell familiar stories, including key details." A very specific retelling rubric may be used to assess students individually three times each year. Yet we also want to monitor students' progress in retelling throughout the year with many different texts. That's where the paper plate rubrics are used.

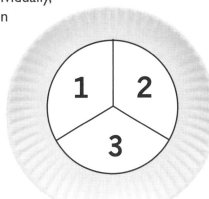

The reproducible on page 104 is a template for a three-point rubric.
You may want to actually write your rubric in each section. Cut out the sections and glue them onto the paper plate.

As students are asked to retell familiar stories, including details, their names are pulled off the posterboard and put on the paper plate in the corresponding section, based on their retelling.

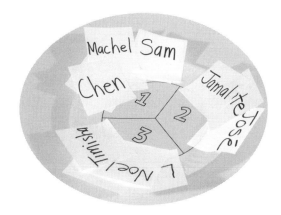

This strategy can be used with just about any concept or strategy you are working with in your classroom. For example Standard RL.K.7 states, "With prompting and support, describe the relationship between illustrations and the story in which they appear (e.g., what moment in a story an illustration depicts)." We are assessing whether or not, with prompting and support, students can describe the relationship between the illustrations and story-line. If yes, their name sticky notes are placed on the top section. If no, their names go on the bottom. The reproducible is on page 105.

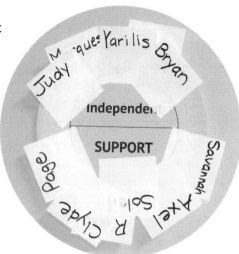

The example below uses a four-point rubric. The reproducible is on page 106.

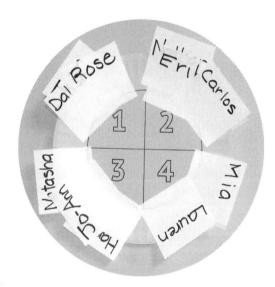

Pair-Share with Assessment Grids

We want our daily assessments to be effective and efficient, but also they should be quick and easy. Assessment grids are one of my favorite formative assessments. Sometimes the information you receive will be more pre-assessment data. You'll see where individual students are in regard to their understanding of new concepts and curriculum being taught.

Sometimes the data is taken in the midst of learning. You'll learn what needs to be retaught and what small flexible groups might be needed. Sometimes the information you receive is at the end of a unit. Then the data grids will be more summative than formative. Grids have allowed me to have the processes of teaching and assessing go hand in hand.

Vygotsky has insisted that "learning is social. Teachers must therefore listen to students to be able to teach, and peers must listen and observe to help each other learn." Often in whole-group settings there are a few students who take over conversations, while others rarely, if ever, are actively involved.

Also, when we present too much information all at once, much of that information is not grasped. If we give our students time to share thoughts with peers as we instruct, most of the critical information is retained. When students talk over new ideas and concepts, their misunderstandings are often revealed during this discussion stage. I also notice that students are more willing to talk when working with a partner rather than in front of the whole class. These assessment grids are used in conjunction with student sharing.

See page 107 for the assessment grid reproducible. On the top of the checklist there is a blank line to write the standard you are assessing. In this example, we are looking at standard RL.K.3: "With prompting and support, identify characters, settings, and major events in a story." The grid has 11 boxes across. Students' names are written in the first box on the left side of the grid, leaving 10 boxes. Each box is worth 10 points so a percentage can be easily calculated. I use checks and minuses. For example, Dajon has one minus and nine checks. This means 90 percent of the time when asked about characters, setting, and major events, he is able to give correct information. Anita has three minuses and seven checks, giving her a percentage of 70 percent on this standard. Michaela can successfully identify the information 60 percent of the time. We are now getting much more information on a daily basis rather than one individual assessment three times a year.

Standard: RL.K. 3: "With prompting and support, identify characters, settings, and major events in a story."

Date(s)

Dajon	✓	✓	✓	−	✓	✓	✓	✓	✓	✓	90%
Anita	−	✓	✓	−	✓	✓	✓	−	✓	✓	70%
Michaela	✓	−	−	✓	✓	✓	✓	−	✓	−	60%

Our goal with all these assessment ideas is to continually let our students' work, conversations, and sharing function as feedback for us to revise our instruction as needed.

Who is the main character?
How would you describe him/her?

How is ____ feeling? Why?

Do you like ____? Why? Why not?

Do you think ____ behaved responsibly?
Why? Why not?

What did ____ do?

What if . . . ?

What happened in the story?

What do you think about . . . ?

What made ____ decide to . . . ?

What part of the book/story was most
interesting or surprising? Why?

What would be another good title for this story? Why?

Where does the story take place?

Where did _____ learn a life lesson in the story?

Where were you confused in the story? Why?

Where in the story did the character get what he/she deserved? Why?

Where in the story was the problem beginning to be solved? Where was it finally solved?

When did the problem get solved?

When did you want to have an argument with _____?

When did you disagree with _____? Why?

When did you agree with _____? Why?

When did . . . ?

When would you have asked _____ to . . . ?

Why do you think . . . ?

Why does _____ feel . . . ?

Why did _____ say . . . ?

Why did ___ do . . . ?

Why did ___ choose . . . ?

Would you recommend this book to a friend?
Why? Why not?

How would . . . ?

How have ___ feelings changed? Why?

How do the characters relate to each other?

How does ___ change in the story?

How does the setting affect the plot of the story?

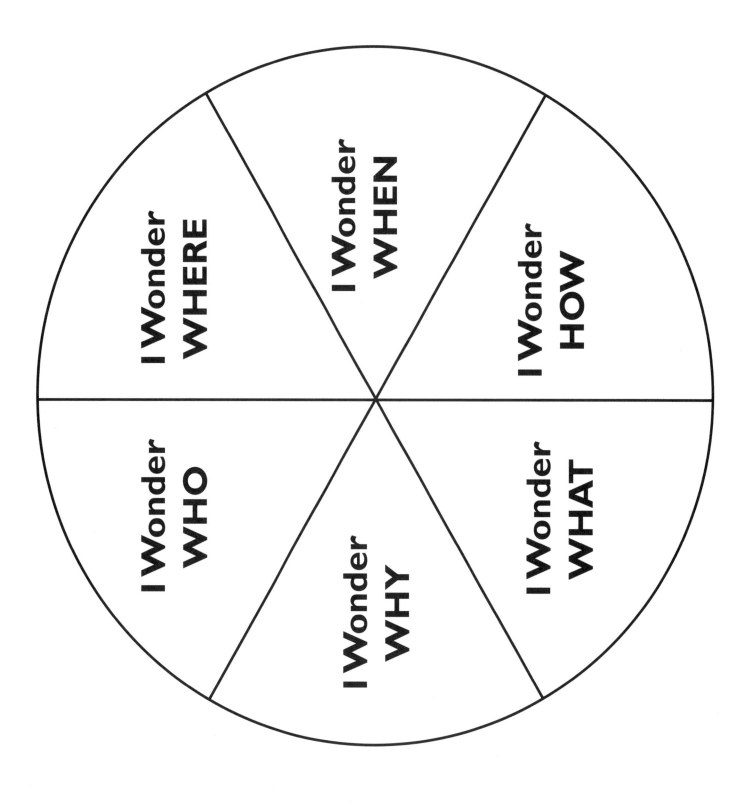

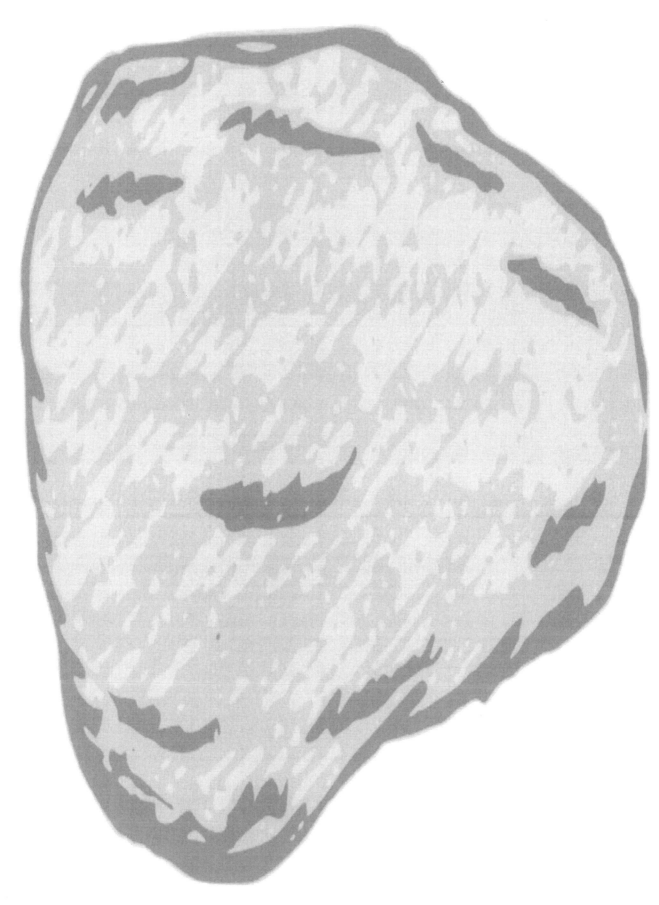

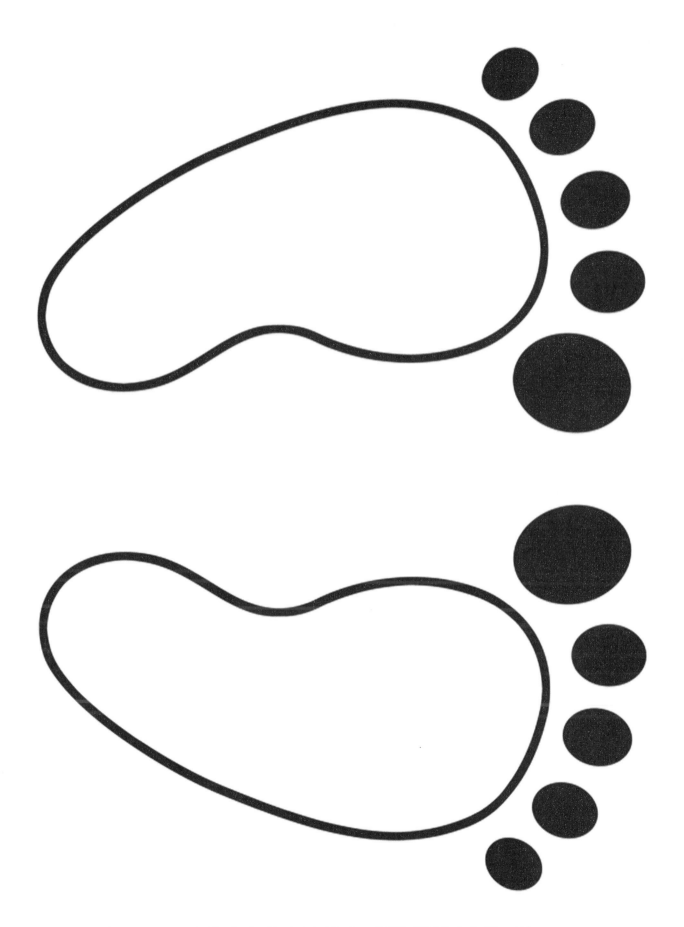

Central Message or Theme

Beginning

Middle

End

Name _____

Title _____

Date _____

The title of the book is

_____

The author is

_____

The illustrator is

_____

My name is

_____

Major events are

The setting is

The characters are

Character's name	What does the character look like?
What does the character like?	**What does the character dislike?**
What is the character's problem?	**What does the character do to solve the problem?**
Describe the character's personality.	**Would you like the character as your friend? Explain.**

Place	**Season**
Time	**See**
Hear	**Smell**
Touch	**Taste**

Name

No! I
Disagree

Yes!
I Agree

Vocabulary Cube

What is a synonym for this word?

Use the word in a sentence about home, school, or you.

Give a definition in your own words.

What is an antonym for this word?

Make a connection to this word. How does this word relate to you?

Why do you think the author used this specific word in the story?

Name

Title

How did you tell us

Illustrator

Author

Name

Title

The illustrator drew ↘

The author wrote

_____
- -
_____
_____
- -
_____
- -
_____
- -
_____

Name

Title

The author wrote

The illustrator showed
this by drawing ↘

Name _____

Title _____

The character's name is

Name _____

Title _____

The setting is

Name _____

Title _____

A major event is

Illustrator

Author

Name

Title

My favorite part
of the story is

(Picture)

Name

Title

My favorite
illustration is

(Picture)

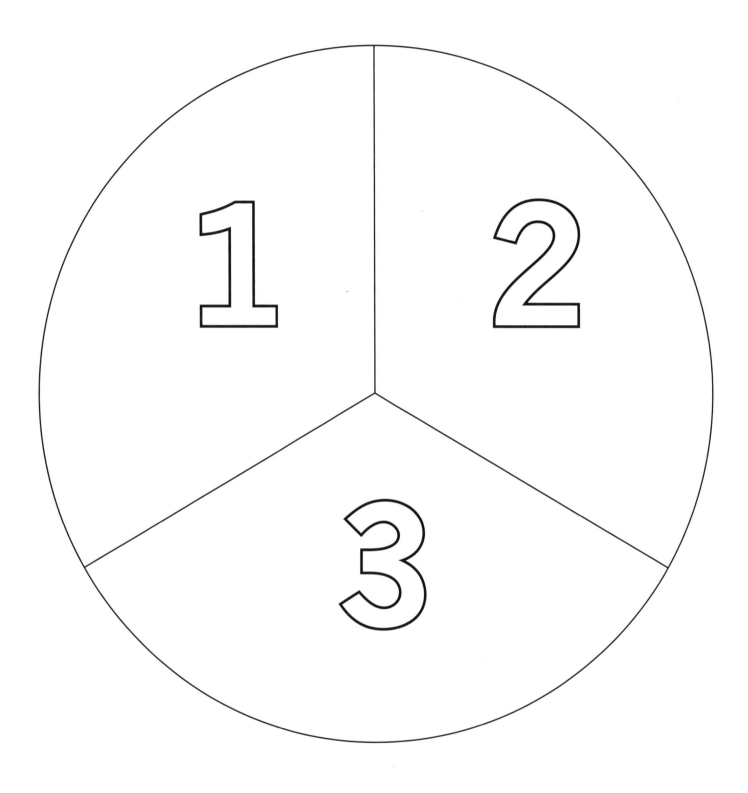

Independent

Support

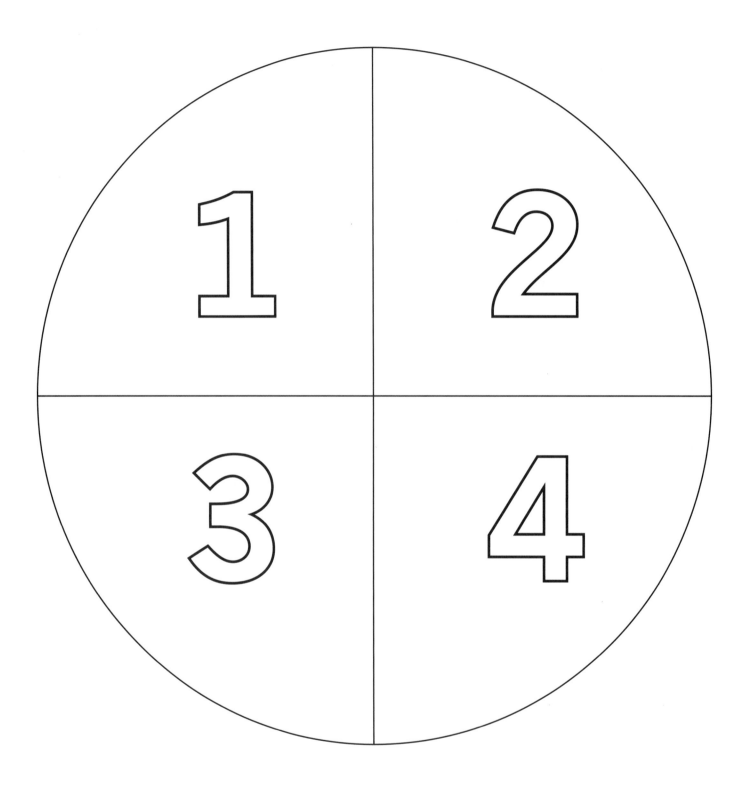

Standard _____

Date(s) _____

Name

Bibliography

Brookhart, Susan M. 2013. *How to Create and Use Rubrics for Formative Assessment and Grading.* Alexandria, VA: ASCD.

Calkins, Lucy, Mary Ehrenworth, and Christopher Lehman. 2012. *Pathways to the Common Core: Accelerating Achievement.* Portsmouth, NH: Heinemann.

Cash, Richard M. EdD. 2011. *Advancing Differentiation.* Minneapolis, MN: Free Spirit Publishing.

Collins, Kathy. 2004. *Growing Readers: Units of Study in the Primary Classroom.* Portland, ME: Stenhouse Publishers.

"Common Core Now What?" December 2012/January 2013. *Educational Leadership.* 70(4).

Cunningham, Andie, and Ruth Shagoury. 2005. *Starting with Comprehension.* Portland, ME: Stenhouse Publishers.

Fyke, Laurie. 2007. *Essential Kindergarten Assessments for Reading, Writing, and Math.* New York: Scholastic.

Gladwell, Malcolm. 2008. *Outliers: The Story of Success.* Boston: Little, Brown.

Guthrie, John T. 2004. *Teaching for Literacy Engagement.* Journal of Literacy Research.

Harvey, Stephanie, and Anne Goudvis. 2007. *Strategies That Work.* Portland, ME: Stenhouse Publishers.

International Reading Association. December 2012/January 2013. *Reading Today: Informed Content for Literacy Professionals* 30(3).

Jago, Carol. 2011. *With Rigor for All* 2nd ed. Portsmouth, NH: Heinemann.

Keene, Ellin Oliver. 1997. *Mosaic of Thought.* Portsmouth, NH: Heinemann.

———. 2008. *To Understand: New Horizons in Reading Comprehension.* Portsmouth, NH: Heinemann.

———. 2012. *Talk About Understanding: Rethinking Classroom Talk to Enhance Comprehension.* Portsmouth, NH: Heinemann.

Kendall, John. 2011. *Understanding Common Core State Standards.* Alexandria, VA: ASCD.

Lipson, Eden Ross. 2000. *Parents Guide to the Best Books for Children.* New York: Three Rivers Press.

Marzano, Robert J., Debra J. Pickering, and Tammy Heflebower. 2011. *The Highly Engaged Classroom.*

Bloomington, IN: Marzano Research Laboratory.

McGill-Franzen, Anne. 2006. *Kindergarten Literacy*. New York: Scholastic Professional Books.

National Governors Association Center for Best Practices (NGA Center) and Council of Chief State School Officers (CCSSO). 2010a. *Common Core State Standards for English Language Arts and Literacy in History/Social Studies, Science, and Technical Subjects*. Washington, DC: NGA Center and CCSSO.

————. 2010b. *Common Core State Standards for English Language Arts and Literacy in History/Social Studies, Science, and Technical Subjects: Appendix A: Research Supporting Key Elements of the Standards; Glossary of Key Terms*. Washington, DC: NGA Center and CCSSO.

————. 2010c. *Common Core State Standards for English Language Arts and Literacy in History/Social Studies, Science, and Technical Subjects: Appendix B: Text Exemplars and Sample Performance Tasks*. Washington, DC: NGA Center and CCSSO.

————. 2010d. *Common Core State Standards for English Language Arts and Literacy in History/Social Studies, Science, and Technical Subjects: Appendix C: Samples of Student Writing*. Washington, DC: NGA Center and CCSSO.

Nye, Barbara, Spyros Konstantopoulos, and Larry Hedges. 2004. *How Large Are Teacher Effects?* Educational Evaluation and Policy Analysis 26 (3;fall): 237–57.

Pavelka, Patricia. 2009. *Differentiating Instruction in a Whole-Group Setting*. East Lyme, CT: Husky Trail Press LLC.

Pinnell, Gay Su, and Irene C. Fountas. 2011. *Literacy Beginnings: A Prekindergarten Handbook*. Portsmouth, NH: Heinemann.

Retelling Tales with Headbands. 2009. City of Commerce, CA: Evan-Moor Educational Publishers.

Rice, Lynda. 2013. *Common Sense Assessment in the Classroom*. Huntington Beach, CA: Shell Education.

Serafini, Frank. 2006. *Lessons in Comprehension: Explicit Instruction in the Reading Workshop*. Portsmouth, NH: Heinemann.

Silver, Harvey F., Thomas R. Dewing, and Matthew J. Perini. 2012. *The Core Six: Essential Strategies for Achieving Excellence with the Common Core*. Alexandria, VA: ASCD.

Taberski, Sharon. 2011. *Comprehension from the Ground Up*. Portsmouth, NH: Heinemann.

Taylor, Barbara. 2010. *Catching Readers Grade 1*. Portsmouth, NH: Heinemann.